Where are our Papas?

By Aaliyah Kopp

Library For All Ltd.

Where are our Papas?

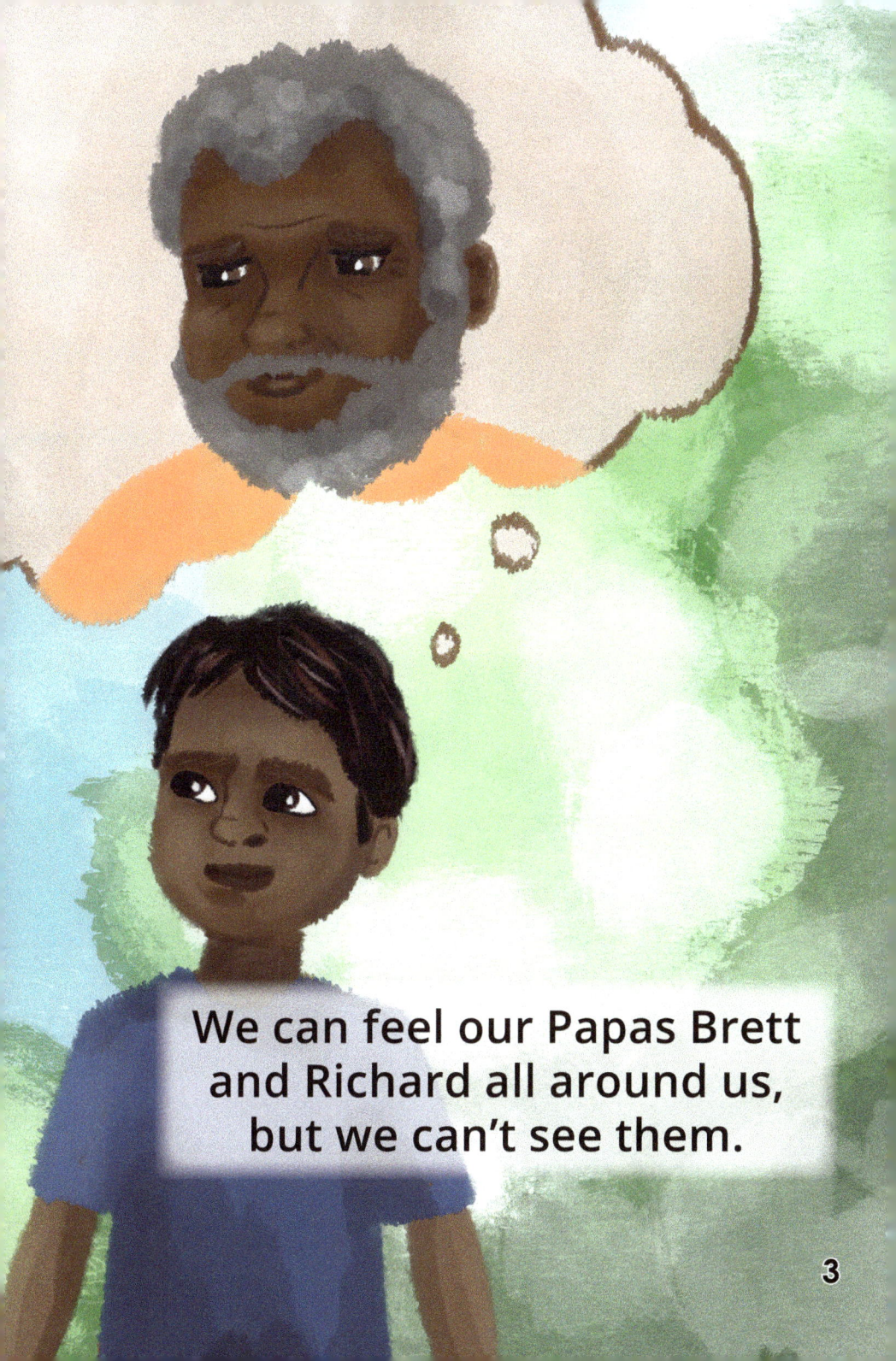

We can feel our Papas Brett and Richard all around us, but we can't see them.

Mummy says they're
in our smiles.

Daddy says they're
in our walk.

Mummy says they're
in our dreams.

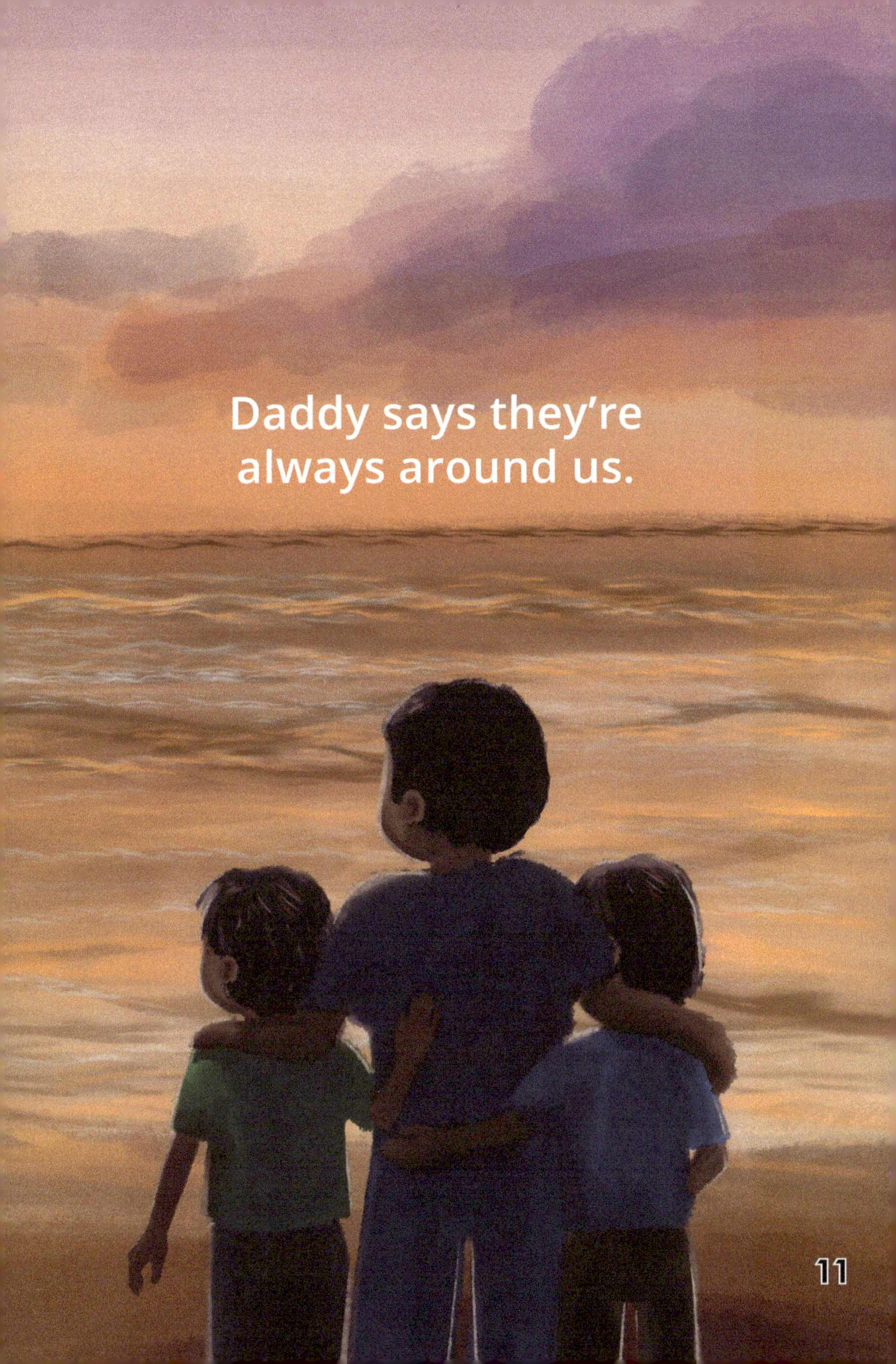

Daddy says they're always around us.

Mummy says they watch over us
high in the sky.

Daddy says they dance and sing
in our dreams.

We wish we could hear and
see them, too.

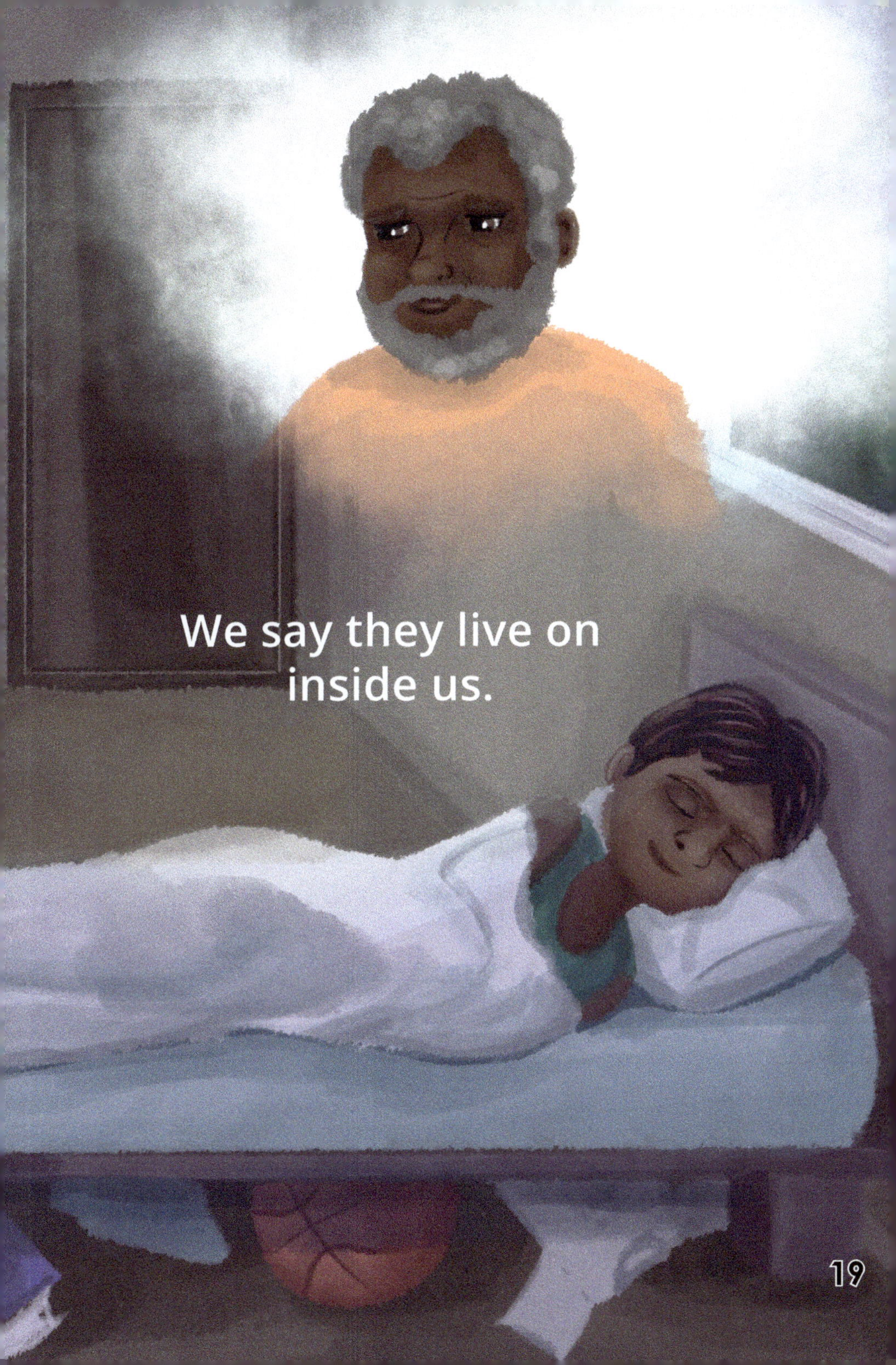

We say they live on
inside us.

You can use these questions to talk about this book with your family, friends and teachers.

What did you learn from this book?

Describe this book in one word. Funny? Scary? Colourful? Interesting?

How did this book make you feel when you finished reading it?

What was your favourite part of this book?

download our reader app
getlibraryforall.org

About the author

Aaliyah is from the Arrernte/Wuthathi Nations and lives in Darwin with her family. Her twin boys keep her busy. She enjoys BBQs, swimming in the ocean, and loved *The Rainbow Fish* as a child.

Our Yarning

Want to discover more books from this collection? Our Yarning is a collection of books written by Aboriginal and Torres Strait Islander peoples across Australia.

We know that children learn better, and enjoy reading more, when they see themselves in the stories, characters and illustrations of the books they read.

To download the app, visit the Google Play Store on any Android device and search 'Our Yarning'.

librisforall.org

www.ingramcontent.com/pod-product-compliance
Lightning Source LLC
Chambersburg PA
CBHW042349040426
42448CB00019B/3471